Young Wildlife

Southern Africa

Young Wildlife

Frolicking and bouncing, tumbling and pouncing, exuberant little spirits are at play under the temperate skies of the African landscape. These are the young mammals of Africa, and like human children, they are at their most content when playing and spend a substantial amount of time and energy doing so. Nevertheless, because nature decrees there must be balance in everything, these young mammals must also learn. Fortunately, they have a great capability of doing this too, and like human children, their minds are at their most absorbent stage and are able to grasp the intricacies of their existence, the skills that will helpfully ensure their survival into adulthood. Unfortunately, this is also the stage when they are at their most vulnerable, and these young mammals are completely dependant on their mothers, and sometimes fathers, for protection and food. Luckily though, with a mother's instinct, these infants are carefully nurtured with months and sometimes years of care, and the great circle of life continues to thrive in this wild and beautiful bushveld.

← A white rhino calf sits dumpishly at his mother's feet, without a horn having grown at this stage, his ungainly and enormous looking feet are his most predominant feature.

↖ One of life's first lessons for the young leopard is to learn to quickly climb into the safety of high branches of a tree. Here they can escape the hungry jaws of a lion, their chief enemy.

↑ The Cape grysbok has single births and lambs can be born at any time of the year, but usually between the months of September and December.

↗ Cheetah cubs with their already characteristic 'tear stained' cheeks, are born blind and helpless and for the first six weeks they are kept hidden in thick undergrowth.

→ After 22 months of gestation, elephant calves are born averagely weighing a rather hefty 120kg. They are a pinkish-grey in colour and are finely covered in hair.

← With the gestation period of a zebra being nearly a year long, the foals are strong and well developed when born, and within the hour they are up and running with the rest of the herd.

↑ Lion cubs are born hidden within a cave or dense cover where predators cannot easily penetrate. These tiny, helpless creatures have a birth weight of approximately only 1kg.

Lion Cub

Lion are the epitome of the "family cat", living in prides of some thirty individuals. The lionesses of the pride will usually conceive at the same time, which has the advantage of an abundance of milk and maternal care for the young cubs.

⇒ Females come into season a few times a year and give birth to between one and four cubs, and on occasion as many as six.

↑ Lion cubs are introduced to the rest of the family at about eight weeks old.

⟵ While it is one of the most common antelope, it is also extremely graceful and beautiful. Impala have single lambs and the newborn impala looks like a miniature version of its mother.

↑ Zebra have one young at a time and the foals form a very close bond with their mothers.

Elephant Calf

Elephant grow up in herds led by a dominant and experienced matriarch, along with several other cows and their young. Of all the mammals, these animals enjoy the longest time of youth.

↑ Calves will accompany their mothers for at least twelve years. Teenage males tend to leave, while females often remain with their birth herd for life, forming lifelong bonds with their mothers.

⇥ Mothers are very caring and protective of their young.

← When baboons are born, they spend the first month clinging to their mother's chest, after that they jump onto her rear and "piggy-back" around. Adult baboons are extremely protective over their young.

↗ Cape fox cubs are usually born in spring, with between one and four in a litter. They live in well-dug underground dens.

⇥ The wild dog is the rarest large carnivore in Southern Africa. From only one month old the pups start to feed on meat by themselves.

Leopard Cub

Although quite abundant, leopard are notoriously shy and elusive creatures, so in turn the discovery of leopard cubs is especially rare.

↖ Their splendid spotted coats are designed for camouflage, rendering them practically invisible in covered territory.

← Newborn young are carefully hidden in impassable dens between rock crevices or dense bush thickets.

↙ Cubs are independent from an early age as they fend for themselves while mom is hunting.

→ Leopard are normally solitary animals, except when accompanied by her young cubs.

← It is a privilege to see baby cheetah, as their mothers hide them carefully in dense grass or bush thickets for the first month of their lives. From an early age they learn the skills of hunting.

→ The rhino cow separates from her group to give birth, and remains separated for a few days with her newborn. For the first few weeks of a baby rhino's life, they are extremely wobbly on their feet.

↑ Hippo mating takes place in the water, but the cow gives birth on the land in dense cover and she and her calf remain separated from her group for several months.

⤳ A mother cheetah is a close companion to her cubs for about eighteen months, after which she leaves them to fend for themselves as she heads off to start a new family

Rhino Calf

Both species of rhino only have single young at birth, and these newborn calves typically weigh around 40kg. The females have calves every three to four years.

← Calves and their mothers stay together for about three years, but when she is ready to give birth again, the mother chases her calf away, a very distressing time for the youngster.

↗ Because the cumbersome and lethargic mothers do not make good playmates, the young rhinos have to entertain themselves.

→ Rhino calves suckle for at least a year, and in that time they grow at a rapid pace.

← Play-fighting is a common ritual for lion cubs, this aids the development of muscles and helps them learn the essential skills for later in life, such as tackling large prey to the ground or fighting off intruders or rivals.

→ The warthog usually gives birth to four piglets. The mother is not afraid to use her sharp tusks to attack even leopards that attempt to kill her young.

Buffalo Calf

Hefty buffalo only inhabit areas with an ample supply of water and grass. They are seasonal breeders, with their calves being born in the rainy season.

← The baby buffalo are quite weak when born, and they take a few hours to adjust to the new world before they are able to follow the herd.

↑ From the start, mothers and calves form a strong bond; they remain close and graze side by side, until she gives birth again approximately two years later.

↖ When lion cubs reach the age of only 3 months, they are taken to a kill, where they are allowed small scraps of meat. However, they still suckle until they are 6 months old.

↑ Baby zebra are particularly playful young animals, especially the male foals, who enjoy springing and cavorting with the other youngsters in the herd.

↗ The delightful suricate mongooses are very playful creatures, even as adults. An average of three pups are born underground in burrows, and are already weaned at the age of two months.

⇢ Baby giraffe are born into the world with a thump – their immensely tall mothers give birth standing up. They are born with small horns that are tipped with a flaming tuft of hair.

← Cheetah cubs are born with a thick fluffy grey mantle. As they grow older, it thins out considerably, but traces of it can still be seen on the top of its head and back.

↑ Foxes and jackals live in mated pairs and are amongst the small group of mammals where the males help to raise their young. Here a Cape fox parent grooms its cub.

← New born antelope [of] all species, including the Cape grysbo[k] [pi]ctured here, are highly developed and a[re]ble to get up and run within a day in orde[r] [to] survive.

Photography - Martin Harvey, R[ic]hard du Toit, Nigel Dennis, Denny Allen, Pe[t]er Chadwick, Roger de la Harpe, Jason K[e]wood, Peter Macfarlane, Andrew McEwan, B [M]cLeod.
Text by Andrea Florens.

Produced by Art Publishers (Pty) Ltd
Durban, Johannesburg, Cape Town